PROPHETIC NUMBERS

30 Day Devotional

Luke Harding

Printed in the United Kingdom
First Printing Edition, 2023
ISBN 9798854941242

Forward

For the last several years, I have seen certain number patterns jump out at me on a regular basis and at key moments. Other believers around me began to say the time thing and I realised that what we were experiencing was not a coincidence.

Numbers such as 1111, 2222, 555 kept showing up and I discovered that there are articles and websites saying the same thing. The only difference is where the numbers are coming from and how they are interpreted.

Some websites describe these numbers as 'angel numbers' which are essentially new age and another form of fortune telling and I would discourage anyone from going on such sites, but that doesn't mean these numbers are wrong in themselves. Remember, the devil cannot create, but he can only imitate or distort what God has already created and made.

He has done this right from the beginning when he twisted the command of God not to eat from the tree of the knowledge of good and evil and led Adam and Eve into disobedience and sin and he continues to pervert God's ways and laws in every possible way even today.

As believers then we need to go to the Holy Spirit and the bible for all our answers including the interpretation of these numerical patterns and that is what I did. I looked up the most relevant verses with the numbers that I was seeing and began to pray over them. For example, 1414 kept coming up and so I discovered Exodus 14:14 was the very word I needed to hear when I saw it. It reads, "The LORD will fight for you; you need only to be still."

Some of the number patterns had meaning as biblical numbers, such as 555, which is a triplicate of 5, the number for grace, while others led me to a key verse that has continued to speak to me and guide me in making the right decisions at the right time, such as 2121, which led me to Matthew 21:21 where Jesus teaches us that we can tell any mountains in our lives to be uprooted by faith.

Numbers play a big role in the bible for God is a God of order and not chaos or chance (1 Corinthians 14:33). Everything He has made is detailed and has a specific plan, purpose and function.

I've been asked on many occasions to shed some light on the reason for certain number combinations that seem to appear for lots of people, so I decided to publish them in this easy-to-read devotional in the hope that it will equip you with some of the scriptures that have helped me and continue to help me at significant times.

My prayer is that they will speak to you as much as they have to me and if you are seeing other numbers on a regular basis then write them down in the back of this book, look up the relevant scriptures and pray into them when they appear.

Prophetic Numbers

DAY 1

1111 – THE PROMISED LAND

But the land you are crossing the Jordan to take possession of is a land of mountains and valleys that drinks rain from heaven.
Deuteronomy 11:11

1111 has been quite a phenomenon over the last decade. There are numerous websites and articles about why people are seeing it so frequently and the majority are from a non-biblical perspective.

We want to hear what God is saying though through this popular combination and the verse that I was led to was Deuteronomy 11:11, which is about God's people crossing over from the wilderness into the Promised Land.

When I see these numbers, it is often during a time of transition as I'm preparing to enter something new and so I thank the Lord that I am crossing over safely into where He has called me, whether it's a new work, ministry, area, relationship or otherwise.

What is in front of us is so much greater than what is behind us, which is why the apostle Paul said in Philippians 3:13-14, "But one thing I do: Forgetting what is behind and straining toward what is ahead, I press on toward the goal to win the prize for which God has called me heavenward in Christ Jesus."

John 11:11 talks about Jesus going to raise Lazarus from the dead and so there is also a connection with resurrection power, awakening and revival, which may be why it is being seen so much more in these times, for we are beginning to see a new great awakening upon the earth, before the Lord returns.

Get ready then to step into all that the Lord is calling you into right now and be expectant of a fresh encounter with Him as you move upward and onward by faith in His Son.

Prayer

Father, when I see 1111, it is a reminder that you want me to cross over into the promises, purposes and plans that you have for me. I also pray for a spiritual awakening and revival in my life that will affect all those around me so that we will see a great move of your Holy Spirit in these last days. In Jesus' name I pray, amen.

DAY 2

2222 – KEYS & OPEN DOORS

I will place on his shoulder the key to the house of David; what he opens no one can shut, and what he shuts no one can open.
Isaiah 22:22

Are you waiting for a door to open in your life? It may be for a relationship, a job, a home or an opportunity to serve God in a greater way. If so, then you need to understand who is able to open that door – Jesus!

When I see 2222, I immediately begin to pray for keys to open doors that need to be unlocked. It may be for fresh revelation or it may be for a chance to share the gospel with someone, but one thing is for sure, Jesus has the key.

Isaiah 22:22 talks about the promotion of a young man in the government called Eliakim who was to be given the large master key of the king's palace, so that he could go anywhere and open and shut any door.

Eliakim is also a prophetic picture of Jesus who has all authority in heaven and earth and holds the keys to Death and Hades, now that He has conquered the grave. The church is reminded in Revelation 3:7 that only Christ can open and close doors and for those who are faithful to Him, a door will be opened that no-one can shut.

We must be able to trust the Lord with the doors that remain closed and thank Him for the ones that open before us. He knows what is best for us even when we don't understand what He is doing.

Let us also not forget that as Christ's ambassadors on the earth, we have been given the keys of the kingdom and now have the authority to bind and loose the spiritual powers around us so that even the demons must submit to us according to Matthew 16:19!

Prayer

Thank you Jesus for every closed and open door. I can trust you completely with my past, present and future. I know that you will open up the way before me as I step forward in faith. Help me to remember the spiritual authority you have given me to bind and loose on the earth, so that I can walk in victory and not defeat. Amen.

DAY 3

333 – REVELATION

Call to me and I will answer you and tell you great and unsearchable things you do not know. Jeremiah 33:3

As Christians, we need revelation as much as we do information. We need to hear from heaven as much as we do from sources on the earth to understand God's perspective. The bible after all is the revealed word of God and ends with a book called Revelation, which describes the finals events of heaven and earth.

The fact is God often wants to speak to us more than we are willing to listen. He knows the way we should take in life and the best decisions to make, and He can save us from a lot of pain, frustration and mistakes if we take the time to hear from Him.

Jeremiah was one of the greatest prophets of his day, yet God still encouraged him to ask for insight and understanding and He wants to give you fresh revelation that will help you and guide you in making right decisions. There are a lot of things we do not know, but God does, and He can reveal them to us at just the right time.

The context of this verse is also encouraging, for Jeremiah was in prison and the nation was about to be judged by God and yet amid all this, the Lord was promising restoration and healing to the people if they would be willing to turn to Him and call on Him again.

This is a great reminder for us also that despite the end-time godlessness we see all around us, we can still reach our heavenly Father with our prayers and see Him answer us and restore us in ways we could never have imagined.

Call on the Lord today and ask Him to show you things that you are unable to see or comprehend in the natural and ask Him to work mightily on your behalf for the sake of His glory.

Prayer

Dear Father, you will not abandon us even in our deepest trials, but instead encourage us to call to you in order to be found by you. I ask for fresh revelation that will help me to understand you better and know the way that I need to take, so that my life can point others to you because of your goodness and love. I pray this in the name of Jesus, amen.

DAY 4

444 – VICTORY ON EARTH

*You are my King and my God, who
decrees victories for Jacob.
Psalm 44:4*

The number 4 has a strong connection with the created world. God finished making the material universe on day 4 of creation. There are also 4 seasons in the year and in Revelation 7:1, John tells us that he "saw four angels standing at the four corners of the earth, holding back the four winds of the earth."

After seeing the numbers 444 and looking it up in the bible, I discovered Psalm 44:4 which talks about God commanding victory for us.

While you and I live on planet earth, we will always be engaged in spiritual warfare with God's enemy and our enemy, the devil. This is the reason why we need to recognise God as both our Lord and King. He wants to protect, defend and fight for us, but He can only do it with our permission.

Make your boast in the Lord alone. Tell yourself and the spiritual powers at war with you that the battle belongs to God and what He has done for His people in the past He can do again, for nothing is impossible for those who trust in Him.

One of the biggest victories in the New Testament came on the 4th day. Jesus was told that Lazarus, one of his closest friends, had died. Instead of rushing to pray for him, Jesus waited until he had been in the tomb for 4 days before he visited him.

This was because Jewish people believed that a person's soul lingered around the body after death for 3 days looking for an opportunity to reenter the person and bring them back to life. After 3 days though there was no going back.

This is the reason why Jesus arrived on day 4. He wanted to show the people that He alone was the "resurrection and the life" and had to power the bring back from the dead and when Jesus died and rose again Himself, His story went to the 4 corners of the earth through 4 eyewitness accounts, which we now call the "gospels."

Declare today that Jesus is Lord and King and will rescue, ransom and redeem you and your family from every demonic attack and battle and will use your victory to show His power to the world.

Prayer

Father, thank you for saving me from the enemy in the past. I believe that you can do it again and so I decree that victory belongs to you and that you are mighty to save. I put my trust in you and ask you to make me a witness of Christ's resurrection power to the world around me. In Jesus' name, amen.

DAY 5

555 – GREAT GRACE

Surely you will summon nations you know not, and nations you do not know will come running to you, because of the Lord your God, the Holy One of Israel, for he has endowed you with splendour.
Isaiah 55:5

The number 5 is all about grace so when I see 555, I pray for great and abundant grace in any situation that I happen to be facing. You see we need God's grace in everything we do in this life. Without His grace, we won't get very far.

I believe our Christian journey starts with grace as the Holy Spirit calls us out of darkness and into the light. We are then saved by grace "through faith—and this is not from yourselves, it is the gift of God" (Ephesians 2:8). Paul said that it was the grace of God that made him who he was and enabled him to work so hard for the gospel (1 Corinthians 15:10).

It's probably no surprise then that God has given us 5 fingers on each hand, 5 toes on each foot and 5 senses in which to operate as human beings on the earth. It's also not surprising that the 10 commandments are made up of 2 sets of 5 and that the anointing oil for the priests is made up of 5 special ingredients.

I was saved at the age of 5 and came to know the grace of God that takes away my sin and makes me a child of God. Now, after nearly 40 years of following Him, I can honestly say that I wouldn't be here today or doing what I am doing without His great and lavish grace upon my life!

We all need grace to know God and live for God and overcome the enemy of our souls. Perhaps that is why the name Christ, meaning "anointed one," is found 555 times in the bible.

One of the verses that stands out in connection with 5 is Isaiah 55:5. It talks about God gathering the nations to Himself through Israel, which is something that we will see in the final millennium, but it is also something the Lord is trying to do now through us as He gathers in the final harvest of souls before the end of the church age.

Prayer

Dear Father, I want to thank you for your grace in and upon my life. I wouldn't be saved without it. Please help me to keep walking in your divine grace and not try to do things in my own strength or through my own works. I pray for great grace especially in times of great trouble and ask you to show your amazing grace to a lost and dying world through me. In Jesus' name, amen.

DAY 6

66 – THE END

And this gospel of the kingdom will be preached in the whole world as a testimony to all nations, and then the end will come.
Matthew 24:14

Did you know there are 66 books of the bible? There are 39 books in the Old Testament and 27 in the New Testament. This brought some relief after seeing 66 so many times. For instead of seeing it as a negative number, I began to view it as a reminder that we are coming to the end of the bible and the end of all things when Jesus will return and we will be with Him forever!

The number 6 itself relates to mankind. The word "mankind" is found 6 times in the bible. Adam and Eve were created on the 6th day. God instructed His people to work for 6 days and rest on the 7th day in honour of Him. The land also was only to be worked for 6 years and then was to remain wild on the 7th year as a year-long Sabbath.

6 also represents the carnal nature of man. The Christian life is a constant struggle between the Spirit and the flesh and we can only live a victorious life in Christ if we "put to death the misdeeds of the flesh" through the power of the Holy Spirit (Romans 8:13). I discovered this as a young man while seeking to live for God and please Him and it is something I still have to keep pursuing today.

When I see 66 now, I realise that it represents the culmination of the age of man. Most people are aware of the infamous 666 mark of the beast described in Revelation 13:16-18 which will come at some point in the tribulation – the last 7 years of earth. I don't believe that we are to dread or fear this as believers though, for we will either be caught up with Jesus before this time or kept from this hour of tribulation in some way.

What's interesting is that while Revelation is the 66th and last book of the bible, Isaiah 66 is the final chapter of the prophet's writings and similarly describes the end of the world: "As the new heavens and the new earth that I make will endure before me," declares the Lord, "so will your name and descendants endure. From one New Moon to another and from one Sabbath to another, all mankind will come and bow down before me," says the Lord. (Isaiah 66:22-23).

Our mission then as end-time believers should for the salvation of lost souls before the window of God's grace closes and night comes when no one can work. 66 reminds us to be actively serving God as much as we can while there is still time left on the earth and to seek opportunities to share His love with others. I pray this for you today.

Prayer

Dear God, please help me to live and operate in the power of the Holy Spirit and to not be controlled and dominated by the flesh. I realise that I can only do this through your grace and power in my life. Help me also to make the most of the time that I have and to always be looking for opportunities to share the gospel and be a light to those around me. In Jesus' name, amen.

DAY 7

777 – TOTAL COMPLETION

When he had received the drink, Jesus said, "It is finished." With that, he bowed his head and gave up his spirit. John 19:30

While 6 is a number that I try to avoid, 7 is one I enjoy seeing and using as much as possible. There is so much to say about 7 that there isn't room enough here to say it, but it's important to know that God put it there at the beginning when He made the world in 7 days and it's there at the end, with the final 7 years of the tribulation period.

7 is all about completion, perfection and rest. The Old Testament priest sprinkled blood 7 times before the Lord and in a similar way, Jesus shed His blood 7 times from Gethsemane to the cross. There are 7 days in a week and the 7th day is one of rest. There were originally 7 divisions of the bible and there are 7 annual holy days or feasts of the Lord, which end in the 7th month of the Hebrew calendar. Paul uses 7 titles for Christ in Hebrews and we are to forgive others 70 x 7 (Matthew 18:21-22).

Seeing 777 reminds me that only God can perfect that which concerns us (Psalm 138:8) and will bring everything to a full completion. Your life might seem broken right now and far from perfection, but the more we fix our eyes on Jesus, the more He will be able to complete us and make us whole.

7 is God's perfect number and should remind us that He has a perfect plan for our lives. Jeremiah 29:11 says: "For I know the plans I have for you," declares the Lord, "plans to prosper you and not to harm you, plans to give you hope and a future." The more I seek the Lord, the more I discover His amazing plan for my life and so can you.

777 is also an indication that the end of all things is fast approaching when every knee will bow and every tongue confess that Jesus Christ is Lord. For we know that the flood in Noah's day, which was an Old Testament sign of the end, came after his father had died at the grand age of 777!

Get ready for an invasion of 7's in these last days. Revelation tells us that there will be 7 angels carrying 7 bowls and blowing 7 trumpets before the end and that there are 7 churches that Jesus addresses, as He walks among 7 golden lampstands while carrying 7 stars and the 7 spirits of God. We also look forward to that final 7th day Sabbath, when we will rest from our labors and be with Jesus forever.

Prayer

Dear Father, thank you for promising to complete everything in my life that is not complete now. I believe that you will perfect everything that concerns me and make me whole. Thank you that Jesus shed His precious blood for me 7 times to bring perfect redemption and salvation and that His 7th and final saying on the earth was "it is finished!". In Jesus' name, amen.

DAY 8

888 – JESUS

And she will bring forth a Son, and you shall call His name Jesus, for He will save His people from their sins. Matthew 1:21

As soon as I began typing up this chapter, I went to pay my tithe for the week. I felt the Lord prompt me to give a specific amount and after I had transferred it, I noticed that there were three 8's all in a row in my remaining balance. Talk about prophetic timing.

888 is the numerical value for Jesus using Gematria, where letters have a corresponding number in the Hebrew alphabet. In fact, other titles for Jesus also include a factor of 8 in them such as Christ, Messiah and Lord. It's a great comfort to see these numbers because we know that Jesus is near and watching over us.

The number 8 is also about a new beginning or new order. There were 8 people that went into the ark and survived the flood in order to repopulate the earth. In the new millennium period, God will expect every inhabitant of the earth to go up to Jerusalem for the Feast of Tabernacles, which is the most joyous feast of all and lasts for 8 days.

8 also represents a new beginning in our faith, for just as Jewish boys were required to be circumcised on the 8th day, we undergo a circumcision of the heart when we are born again of the Holy Spirit. I don't believe it was a coincidence that Jesus is recorded as

having appeared 8 times after His resurrection, for again it's proof that we too will enter a new state when we are resurrected to new life for all eternity.

It doesn't matter what your background is or what you've done in life, Jesus wants to give you a fresh start and new beginning through His precious blood. Romans 10:13 says, "Everyone who calls on the name of the Lord will be saved." I've had the privilege of helping lots of different people call on Jesus and invite Him into their hearts.

If this is something that you have never done then I want to encourage you to surrender your life to Christ today so that He can give you new life in abundance as He promised in John 10:10. If you want to do this then pray the following prayer as an invitation to let God into your heart:

Prayer

Dear God, I believe that you sent Jesus to die on the cross for my sins and in my place. I'm sorry for living my life without you and for going in a different direction. I choose to put my trust in your Son from today and follow Him for the rest of my life. Please help me to live for you and baptize me with your Holy Spirit. In Jesus' name, amen.

DAY 9

0909 – GOD'S APPOINTED TIME

For this was how the promise was stated: "At the appointed time I will return, and Sarah will have a son."
Romans 9:9

We must remember that life is not random and events do not happen merely by chance, but God is a creative and intentional Father who loves us and has arranged everything according to His master plan and schedule. There is an end-date to our suffering and trials and there are marked days for our deliverance and breakthrough.

The Lord promised Abraham that he would have a son and heir even in his old age and that it would be a miracle, since his body was as good as dead in terms of procreation. There was also a day set aside especially for this promise to come to pass and there are appointed times for us also to see God's word come to fruition.

I prayed for many years to serve God in a full-time capacity until the time came for the answer in early 2020, which was nearly 2 decades after I had originally left Bible College. Thankfully, the Lord knew that I needed these years to develop my character and faith, so that I would be better equipped to carry the weight of the calling when He eventually released me.

You might be praying for something to come to pass in your life today or for an answer to a certain need and you might be tempted to think that God hasn't heard you or that it will never happen, but you must remember there are appointed times for us set in heaven and that they will come at the right time. Our job is to stay in peace and to continue trusting Him until He does it.

There are set times for you, for your family, for this world and for Jesus' return and we can rest knowing that these times are perfect.

Prayer

Dear Lord, I know from Psalm 31:15 that "my times are in your hands" and nothing will happen to me outside of your foreknowledge and will. I thank you that your promises will come to pass at just the right time, whether it is for me personally or for the wider body of Christ and so I continue to trust in your perfect timing and plan. In Jesus' name, amen.

DAY 10

1010 – ABUNDANT LIFE

The thief comes only to steal and kill and destroy; I have come that they may have life, and have it to the full.
John 10:10

A few years ago, the Lord called me to go into the city and start sharing the gospel to as many people as possible. As I stepped out, another group of believers simultaneously did the same and together we held worship and evangelism outreaches in various places, sowing seeds and leading people to Jesus. The name of their group was John 10:10 and it's a number I've seen many times.

Jesus came to the earth with one express purpose and that was to bring life as we read in this verse. He brought life to sick bodies, tormented souls and troubled minds and ultimately released eternal life to all those who would believe in Him and accept His atoning sacrifice at the cross.

One translation reads 'abundant' life and the Greek word for this means an extraordinary, superabundant, above and beyond life. This is God's will and plan for us – to be so filled with the Holy Spirit that we overflow with love, peace, righteousness, hope and joy.

The devil on the other hand seeks to bring the opposite. His only aim is to 'steal, kill and destroy' peoples' lives and sadly we can see this in operation all around us in the world. When people don't follow God's plan and try to live without Him then they become open prey for the devil to come and rob them of all that is good.

The good news is that we don't have to be sitting ducks for the enemy but can tap into the overflowing life of Jesus and we can do this through our confession. Proverbs 18:21 says, "The tongue has the power of life and death, and those who love it will eat its fruit." What comes out of our mouths will determine the quality and outcome of our lives.

Decide today to start speaking faith-filled, life-giving words over yourself, your family, your church, your work and your nation and watch the change that it will bring for good.

Prayer

Father, thank you for sending Jesus into this world to give me life. You don't just want us to survive, but you want us to thrive in every area. I choose today to intentionally release words of life to every situation around me knowing that it will bring a great harvest when I do. I declare that I will walk in your abundant life and help others to do the same. In Jesus' name, amen.

DAY 11

1122 – ASKING GOD

But I know that even now God will give you whatever you ask. John 11:22

One day, I received a text message that presented me with a challenge and threatened a good kingdom relationship. I immediately gave it to God and prayed with Pahline, my mother, who runs the ministry with me. The next day, God miraculously made a way through the difficulty and the friendship was saved. I then looked at the time and it was 11:22 – a number I had seen before and which lead me to the very verse that summed up what we had done, which was to ask God for help.

Too often, we go to everyone and everything else when faced with a crisis or problem, rather than going directly to God. He is the only one who can truly help us in times of trouble and who can answer our requests when we call to Him, which is why He encourages us to bring our requests to His throne.

The context of this verse in John 11 was that Lazarus had died and had been in the tomb for 4 days by the time Jesus arrived. Martha felt that Jesus had come too late, but at the same time, continued to believe that anything was possible through Him, which is why she said, "even now, God will give you whatever you ask."

There are times when we too face an 'even now' situation. It may be a relationship that looks unrepairable or a physical complaint that seems hopeless. It might look like it's over in the natural, but nothing is impossible for God even when it looks impossible for us.

The key is to trust in the Lord one more time and ask Him to do what no one else can do. Jesus not only died for us on the cross but is now at the Father's right hand in heaven interceding for us so that we will not fail but be victorious in Him.

Go to the Saviour today and let Him take you to the Father, who already knows what you need and how to bring it about.

Prayer

Dear Father, even if my situation looks hopeless, impossible or beyond remedy, there is still hope with you. I choose to ignore the outward appearance of what I am facing and instead look to your wonder-working power that is available in Jesus today. In His mighty name, amen.

DAY 12

1212 – DIVINE ORDER

For God is not a God of disorder but of peace—
as in all the congregations of the Lord's people.
1 Corinthians 14:33

The number 12 is all about God's authority and divine kingdom order. It also symbolizes the nation of Israel as a whole. Whenever I see 1212, I pray for God's sovereign order and rule in any given situation for it is part of the Lord's prayer when Jesus told us to pray: "your kingdom come, your will be done, on earth as it is in heaven" (Matthew 6:10).

God is interested in every detail of our lives however big or small. Everything He has done since the creation of the world has been with a design, purpose and order. He leaves nothing to chance but incorporates all things into His divine plan from the beginning of our lives to the end. It's why Paul was able to say with confidence that "in all things God works for the good of those who love him, who have been called according to his purpose" (Romans 8:28).

Whenever we see the number 12 it should remind us of God's kingdom order for Israel and the church. The nation of Israel was founded on 12 tribes and the church was built on the foundation of the 12 apostles who witnessed everything Jesus did and spoke. In Revelation 4, we are told that there are 24 elders (2x12) seated on thrones with gold crowns on their heads, surrounding God's throne.

I was 12 years old when I got baptised and it marked a significant milestone in my faith. Jesus was 12 years old when He famously spoke to the rabbinical teachers of the law in the temple at Jerusalem. In Luke 8, Jesus heals a woman who has had a blood issue for 12 years and then immediately visits a 12-year-old girl who has just died and raises her up. These powerful miracles were further proof of His divine power and authority!

You need to know that you are not here by accident – God knew you while you were still in your mother's womb and has a good plan for the rest of your life, no matter what you've experienced or gone through up till now. Ask Him to bring order and completion to those areas that are broken and incomplete, for as we've seen, it's God's desire to work all things together for good.

Prayer

Dear Lord, please perfect that which concerns me as promised in Psalm 138:8 and establish your divine order and kingdom rule into my life. I don't want to live in chaos or disorder any longer. I pray this for the nations of the world also that you would bring an end to the broken government of this world and usher in your new millennial reign with Christ as King. In Jesus' name, amen.

DAY 13

0613 – RESISTING SIN

Therefore, put on the full armour of God, so that when the day of evil comes, you may be able to stand your ground, and after you have done everything, to stand. Ephesians 6:13

This is a significant number and one which I've seen many times. Firstly, it contains the number 6 which is related to man apart from God, and secondly, it ends with 13 which is connected to rebellion and sin. Overall then it is a number dealing with sin and separation from God.

The Jewish Talmud points out 613 commandments in the Torah and divides it into 365 negative ones (days in the solar year) and 248 positive ones (number of believed bones and main organs in the body at that time). The commandments of God were given to highlight sin and show Israel how to live righteously, but they could never be perfectly followed, so sin remained.

It is only through believing on Jesus and what He did on the cross in atoning for our sin and shame that we can be made righteous before God. Observing the law will never save us; it only serves to point out what we are doing wrong.

The New Testament reveals 3 steps that we can take to avoid sin and temptation and to be able to stand and not fall.

The first step is prayer. Matthew 6:13 is one of the last parts of the Lord's prayer and says, "And lead us not into temptation, but deliver us from the evil one." While we are in the world, the devil will use things to pull us away from God which is why we need to pray and ask Him to keep us on the right path and to protect us from demonic forces stronger than us.

The second step is consecration. Romans 6:13 warns us "Do not offer any part of yourself to sin as an instrument of wickedness, but rather offer yourselves to God." Consecration is when we give something over to be used. We should give our lives over to God for His purposes.

The third step is to put on God's armour. Ephesians 6:13 tells us to "put on the full armour of God, so that when the day of evil comes, you may be able to stand your ground, and after you have done everything, to stand." After we have offered ourselves to the Lord, we must get covered by Him and His spiritual armour to be able to stand against sin and temptation.

Prayer

Dear Lord, please continue to keep me from sin and wrongdoing and to help me stand against the enemies' traps and attacks. I cannot make myself righteous by what I do or don't do, but I am only saved by my faith in the blood of Jesus Christ. The devil roams around like a roaring lion, but I know I can resist him as I humble myself before you. In Jesus' name, amen.

DAY 14

1414 – GOD WILL DELIVER US

The Lord will fight for you, you need only to be still. Exodus 14:14

1414 has been one of the numbers that we have seen the most and have needed the most as we have pioneered forward for the kingdom. Every time we see it, we declare out loud that the Lord will fight for us as we strive to stay at peace according to Exodus 14:14. Usually when this number pops up, it's because we need to be reminded of God's saving power in our situation!

The number 14 coincidentally represents deliverance and salvation. It was on the 14th day of the first month that the Israelites were released from over 400 years of slavery in Egypt and it was on the 14th day of the first month that Jesus died for our sins as the perfect Passover lamb. Jesus was also born after 3 sets of 14 generations, beginning with Abraham, as recorded in Matthew 1.

One of the most testing times of my life was in 2013, but in the same year I also experienced a major breakthrough which caused the 14th year to be a special one of freedom and hope and prophetically I had just moved into a property that was number 14.

Jesus wants to save and deliver us from every attack of the enemy, whether it is a recent ambush or a long-standing generational issue. Part of the key to victory is "to be still" as Exodus 14:14 points out. This doesn't mean we need to take a passive position of inactivity though, but rather we need to get into a place of peace and confidence in God that no matter how dire the situation looks, the Lord is still in control and will come to rescue us.

We've had to do this many times throughout our Christian lives and we are still putting it into practice today. Stress, anxiety, worry and fear does not speed our breakthrough or freedom. If anything, it blocks the Holy Spirit from fully operating on our behalf, but when we surrender our fears and worries to the Lord, He is turn it around faster than we can.

The number 14 is also 7x2 and so indicates a double perfection or completion. I believe that no matter how long you have been praying for God to bring you out of a situation or trial, His promises never fail and at just the right time they will be fulfilled.

Prayer

Father, thank you for your promise of victory and freedom. Thank you that just as you delivered the Israelites from centuries of Egyptian slavery and bondage, you are also able to deliver me from everything that troubles and afflicts me today. I declare that I am breaking out of every chain and coming into the freedom that Christ died to give me. I choose to trust you in this and keep at peace. In Jesus' mighty name, amen.

DAY 15

0515 – HEALING & FORGIVENESS

And the prayer offered in faith will make the sick person well; the Lord will raise them up. If they have sinned, they will be forgiven.
James 5:15

The number patterns and corresponding scriptures in this devotional are not set in stone but are the verses that the Lord has used to speak to me and hopefully will speak to you. I would encourage you to look up other verses relating to numbers you see on a regular basis. I believe God will speak to you through them. At the very least, it is helping us to study God's word which is always beneficial.

I discovered James 5:15 after having seen 05:15 and it reminds us that Jesus came to heal us and forgive us. It is the dual power of the cross and validates Psalm 103:2-3 that sings, "Praise the Lord, my soul, and forget not all his benefits—who forgives all your sins and heals all your diseases."

We should be fully convinced that the Lord wants to heal our bodies and cleanse our souls. Jesus didn't just die to save us from sin, but he was beaten and crushed so that we could be made fully whole in every way. Those who deny healing are missing out on such a great promise and gift.

As pastors, we have put this into practice over the years and have prayed for people and anointed them with oil according to James 5:14 and we have seen the Lord heal all sorts of issues and complaints including cancers, viruses, heart conditions, breathing difficulties, mental issues and much more.

If you need prayer for healing, I'd encourage you to go to your leaders and ask them to do this for you, believing that you will be restored to health and forgiven as they pray.

Prayer

Dear Father, please increase my faith to believe that nothing is impossible for you and nothing is irreversible or incurable. Thank you for healing me and saving me from all sin, sickness and shame. I refuse to hold onto anything that Jesus died to destroy and look to the cross afresh today for total victory. In Jesus' name, amen.

DAY 16

0616 – CROSSROADS

This is what the LORD says: "Stand at the crossroads and look; ask for the ancient paths, ask where the good way is, and walk in it, and you will find rest for your souls."
Jeremiah 6:16

We all come to a point in our lives where we need to make big decisions for the future. It might be what career to take, what area to live in, or what person to marry. Each time, it's like coming to a crossroads where we need to choose a path to follow.

I remember coming to the end of my master's degree in Edinburgh and wanting to keep studying by pursuing a doctorate in Oxford. At the time, I was convinced this was the right move, but as I tried to go forward with the application nothing seemed to go right. I took time out to seek God and He led me instead to go and support my parents in running their new church plant in the North of England.

This proved to be the right move for me at that time and I've never looked back in regret for not pursuing a doctorate in Theology. God certainly had a different path for me and it was the best one I could have taken for everything fell into place when I followed it.

When I see 0616, it reminds me of the passage above in Jeremiah, where God advises the nation of Israel to seek Him for the right direction which will bring blessing and peace.

If you are standing at a crossroads right now, I would encourage you to seek God about which way to take. We don't know the outcome of the choices before us, but He does, and He can keep us from making wrong and unnecessary mistakes if we are willing to listen to Him. It's easy to be steered by family, friends, circumstances and needs, but it's better to be led by the Holy Spirit for He will never let us down.

Remember also those in the world who are standing at the crossroads of life. Jesus told us to invite them to His great wedding feast in Matthew 22:9 and we can do this by sharing the gospel and showing them what Christ has done for us. We did this for a couple of years when we evangelised at a busy intersection in the city, which was aptly called 'Great Junction Street!'

Prayer

Dear Father, thank you for showing me the way to take whenever I come to a crossroads in life. I don't always know the best decisions to make, but you do and promise to lead and guide me in the way that I should go. I submit myself to you and trust in your divine guidance and plan. I also pray for those who don't know you to choose to follow Jesus and find rest for their souls. In His name, amen.

DAY 17

1717 – HELPERS

A friend loves at all times, and a brother is born for a time of adversity.
Proverbs 17:17

As the poem goes, "no man is an island" and this is especially true in the kingdom of God. We were never meant to navigate through life on our own, but we were saved and adopted into a new heavenly family and can expect help from others along the way.

All throughout my life, God has graciously put the right people around me at the right time. Even at my birth, there happened to be a Christian mid-wife assisting my mother during a long and difficult delivery, refusing to leave her side until I had fully entered the world.

This is not to say that I've never felt alone or surrounded by the wrong people, but when I have sought God for help and asked Him for the right person in my life, He has usually come through.

For example, at the age of 15, I began to get serious in living for Jesus and prayed for a Christian friend for I knew lots of people from school but didn't have anyone who shared my beliefs. Shortly after praying this, we joined a new church and I met Ben who was the same age as me and enjoyed the same things as myself! We became a rap duo called 'Rapture' and together rapped, evangelised and travelled across London, meeting other Christians and sharing our faith.

When we look at the life of the early church it was all about family and working and praying together. It was never about lone individuals, refusing to connect to the wider body of Christ. Even when Christians did find themselves isolated, like Paul in prison or John on the Isle of Patmos, the Lord would send help and relief either in the form of other believers or through angels or Jesus Himself.

Prayer

Dear Father, it can often feel lonely trying to live for you in this world, but I know that I am never alone and that you are always with me. Please release the right people I need in my life today in order to carry out your purposes and plans and who can help me grow in my faith and become more like you. I pray this in Jesus' name, amen.

DAY 18

1818 – BINDING & LOOSING

"Truly I tell you, whatever you bind on earth will be bound in heaven, and whatever you loose on earth will be loosed in heaven."
Matthew 18:18

I've seen 1818 a good number of times and I've also implemented Matthew 18:18 many times and seen it work.

As believers, we have been commissioned to carry on the work of Jesus through the power of the Holy Spirit here on the earth. This means we should be walking in the authority of Christ and allowing what He would allow and disallowing what He would disallow.

Too often, the church operates as if it has no real power or authority and just lets people and events take place without challenging it or confronting it. Jesus said that we have the keys of the kingdom at our disposal and should be administering the plans of heaven upon the earth.

As pastors, we've probably lost count of the number of times that we have taken authority over people, problems or situations, but when we have done it in alignment with God's word and will, it has always worked. Any believer can do this, if they are walking with the Lord and know their identity in Him.

Part of our mission is to take authority over the forces of darkness that try to operate in our families, churches, communities and nations. We should never just accept sin or wickedness as a consequence of fallen man, but should be looking to address anything which conflicts with the righteousness of God.

Over the years, we have bound up anti-Christ spirits, Jezebel spirits, rebellion and witchcraft. We have bound up unclean spirits from attacking our young people and at the same time have loosed and released angels to fight for us and those being saved.

You have the keys to victory today in the power and authority of Christ within you. Don't let the devil push you around or intimate you but take authority over him and his evil plans.

Prayer

Dear Lord, thank you that you have empowered me to take control of situations that are not of your will. I refuse to passively sit back and let the enemy do what he wants to do. You have called me to make a change, to stand in the gap and to administer your justice and righteousness wherever I go. Show me what to bind and loose I pray. In Jesus' name, amen.

DAY 19

1919 – RULING OVER CITIES

"His master answered, 'You take charge of five cities.'" Luke 19:19

I remember listening to a respected preacher talk about how God took him to heaven and showed him a city being prepared there for a famous evangelist who had served the Lord for many decades and how he had the unexpected opportunity to share the vision with him. It reminded me of Jesus' parable in Luke 19:19 where a noble goes away to become king and entrusts 10 minas (around 3 months wages) to 10 of his servants while he is gone.

The servants are told to put the money to work until the master returns and when he does, he calls them to come and give an account of what they have done with it. The first servant says that he has made 10 more, while another says he has made 5 more. They are then rewarded with 10 cities and 5 cities respectively. Now that's a return on their investment!

God has given each of us talents and gifts in equal measure to use for His kingdom. The question is, are we putting to work what He has entrusted to us? One day we will have to give an account of what we have done for the Lord with what He gave us and we will be rewarded accordingly.

I believe that cities and towns will be part of God's reward to us, as well as other responsibilities and titles. The bible teaches us that we are co-heirs with Christ and we go where He goes and we do what He does. If Christ is coming back to the earth to rule as King, then I believe we will also reign with Him as His people. Revelation 1:6 and 5:10 confirms this.

Even writing and publishing this devotional is a way of multiplying what God has shown me to others and I believe that many of you reading this also have dreams and plans to write, sing, serve, minister and lead and I pray that you will have the strength, courage and grace to put it into action from today.

We certainly don't want to be like the servant who hid the mina away and did nothing with it, for it was taken away from him and given to the one with 10 minas! Instead, we want to utilise and maximise everything we have been given so that we can expect to hear the words "well done, good and faithful servant" (Matthew 25:23).

Prayer

Father, thank you for what you have given me and entrusted to me. I want to use my gifts, talents and opportunities for your kingdom and see them multiply and increase. I refuse to hide or bury what you have put inside of me, either out of fear, apathy or indifference. I believe that what we do for you will be rewarded when you return. In Jesus' name, amen.

DAY 20

2020 – BREAKTHROUGH

Early in the morning they left for the Desert of Tekoa. As they set out, Jehoshaphat stood and said, "Listen to me, Judah and people of Jerusalem! Have faith in the LORD your God and you will be upheld; have faith in his prophets and you will be successful."
2 Chronicles 20:20

I think it's fair to say that 2020 was a year the world will never forget when it went into global lockdown due to a coronavirus pandemic. There had been great expectation and excitement as we entered a new decade only to find ourselves in a position no-one had anticipated.

For many believers though, myself included, 2020 was a breakout year. I remember feeling stirred in my spirit in the latter half of 2019 to get ready for what God was going to do. This led me into greater prayer and focus and in January 2020, it happened.

While running my business at that time, the Lord clearly spoke to me and said, "you're coming out of hiding!" I had been serving in the church up until then but with no online or global influence. When I received this word, I knew that He was calling me into full-time ministry and that it was a word for other people as well.

I recorded a short video of myself sharing this word and uploaded it to my YouTube channel which had less than 10 subscribers at the time. The video began to go viral and people were messaging me to say that the word was also for them. By March 2020, just before the lockdown, I had laid down my business and stepped into full-time ministry by faith.

During this year, there were others also who took up the call of God and moved into new kingdom positions. I saw God raise up new leaders who continued to preach the word of God and refused to be cowered or intimidated by world events.

Sometimes great challenges are an opportunity for great breakthroughs – just look at David facing and defeating Goliath as a teenage boy! If you are facing an enemy today, like Jehoshaphat in 2 Chronicles 20:20, look to God and believe in His word that He will never fail you or forsake you and instead see it as an opportunity for divine breakthrough and advancement.

Prayer

Dear Father, while the world panics and frets at the different crises going on right now, I choose instead to see the opportunity in serving you and showing others how great you are. Help me to advance with fresh boldness and courage and to step into all you have called me to, believing for spiritual success and breakthrough as I do. In Jesus' name, amen.

DAY 21

2121 – MOVING MOUNTAINS!

Jesus replied, "Truly I tell you, if you have faith and do not doubt, not only can you do what was done to the fig tree, but also you can say to this mountain, 'Go, throw yourself into the sea,' and it will be done." Matthew 21:21

We see 2121 come up quite regularly and every time we do we begin to speak to the spiritual mountains in our lives that are standing in our way as Jesus told us to in Matthew 21:21.

Mountains can come in all different forms. It may be a mountain of ill-health, debt, relationship issues, mental torment and so forth. It is basically anything that looms over us, blocks us or tries to intimate us. God wants to lead us on level paths and promises in Isaiah 45:2 to move these problems out of the way for those He has chosen: "I will go before you and will level the mountains."

We need faith though in order to speak to the mountains in our lives and we must keep speaking to them until they are fully removed.

A man in our church, who had only been saved for a short time, put this into practice. He had a beloved dog that had developed a large tumour, but instead of accepting the worse and putting the dog down, he began to the speak to the tumour and commanded it to be uprooted and thrown into the nearby lake. He continued to do this until the unsightly growth eventually shrivelled to nothing!

Your mountain might be different to mine, but we both serve the same God and can exercise the same faith to see it removed. Do not be discouraged if you don't see immediate results; sometimes mountains must be broken up over time.

In Isaiah 41:15, God says to Israel and to us: "See, I will make you into a threshing sledge, new and sharp, with many teeth. You will thresh the mountains and crush them and reduce the hills to chaff." I can personally testify to this verse for I have continued to chip away at problems, challenges and strongholds with the help of the Holy Spirit have seen them eventually disappear and I believe you can do same if you persist in telling your mountain that it has to move!

Prayer

Dear Father, thank you for the promise that we can speak to the mountains in our lives and see them removed forever. I choose to walk in faith today and not fear and will continue to uproot every encumbering spirit and obstacle that stops me walking in the plans that you have for me. In Jesus' name, amen.

DAY 22

222 – MIRACLES, SIGNS & WONDERS

"Fellow Israelites, listen to this: Jesus of Nazareth was a man accredited by God to you by miracles, wonders and signs, which God did among you through him, as you yourselves know." Acts 2:22

My mother Pahline, a co-founder of our ministry, pointed out one of the meanings for this number combination. She highlighted Acts 2:22 and noted that it is one of the few places in the bible where "miracles, signs and wonders" are all referenced together.

Jesus told us that we would do greater things than He Himself had done on the earth in John 14:12, which in some ways is hard to fathom, but even now people are seeing incredible miracles take place around the world.

It's not for an elite few to see these supernatural wonders either, but for the whole body of Christ, if we believe in Him. He wants us to step out by faith and expect to see heaven come down to earth in amazing ways and we've certainly seen God do incredible things over the years, from healing to divine provision to turnaround in people's lives.

You do not need to be a pastor, evangelist or gifted speaker to see the miraculous take place – you just need to believe that the same power that raised Christ from the dead lives in you and that God wants to use you to do greater things in these days.

Look for opportunities to pray for people and show the world that there is hope for what they are facing right now through the wonder-working power of the Lamb.

Prayer

Dear Father, please use me to be a vessel for your glory in these days. I believe that signs and wonders will follow me as I step out in faith and declare your word. Lead me to those who need a miracle from heaven today. In Jesus' name, amen.

Day 23

2323 – Divine Protection

There is no divination against Jacob, no evil omens against Israel. It will now be said of Jacob and of Israel, 'See what God has done!'
Leviticus 23:23

Do you remember when Balaam tried to curse Israel? His planned attack was turned into words of blessing every time he opened his mouth. Proverbs 16:7 says, "When the LORD takes pleasure in anyone's way, he causes their enemies to make peace with them." We should not expect evil curses or trouble to overtake us while we are walking with the Lord and the Holy Spirit.

There is a divine canopy and force-field around the righteous that will keep out demonic attacks and infiltration. This is not to say that we are exempt from trials and tests, but generally we are kept in the shelter of God's wings and when trouble does come our way, the Lord is our deliverer and will rescue us from every evil attack.

As pastors for nearly 2 decades, we have noticed that those who stay in church, attend regularly and are spiritually connected to the body, come under a supernatural protection from God. Those who step out of church fellowship and try to face life on their own, quickly come out of this blessing and become open to all sorts of problems and attacks.

According to Job 1:10, there is an invisible hedge or wall of protection around God's people – around their finances, families, hearts, souls, minds, possessions and the enemy is always looking for a way to penetrate this barrier. It's why 1 Peter 5:8 says, "the devil prowls around like a roaring lion looking for someone to devour."

It is also why the bible tells us to guard our hearts above all things (Proverbs 4:23) and to not give him a foothold through sin, unforgiveness or anger.

If you are obeying God's commands and seeking to do what is right before Him, you can expect to walk in the blessings of Deuteronomy 28 and be covered from all the fiery darts of the evil one. If you have sinned or gone off course then repent before God and come back under the powerful protection of the blood of Jesus.

Prayer

Dear Father, thank you for continually watching over my life and for protecting me from the attacks of the enemy. I declare that a causeless curse cannot land on my family. I choose to stay under the shadow of your wings and abide in the shelter of the Most High where no foe can reach. In Jesus' name, amen.

DAY 24

0404 – THE LIVING WORD

Jesus answered, "It is written: 'Man shall not live on bread alone, but on every word that comes from the mouth of God.'"
Matthew 4:4

Jesus knew the importance of God's word. After 40 days of fasting in the wilderness, He was tempted by the devil to turn stones into bread in order to give in to His hunger. His response was to remind the tempter that God's word is even more important that food itself with a quote from Deuteronomy 8:4.

Food is necessary and we need it to stay alive, but the same is true of the bible. We need to regularly read and digest it in order to feed and nourish our souls. Psalm 19:11 describes God's commands as "sweeter than honey, than honey from the honeycomb." If we neglect the bible, we will become spiritually malnourished and our faith will be affected as a result.

God promised Joshua that he would be prosperous and successful if he kept the "Book of the law" always on his lips, meditated on it daily and was careful to follow it (Joshua 1:8) and the same is true for us today. Reading and studying the bible will keep us on the right path and save us from error.

Even as a young boy, I had an appreciation for God's word. While in primary school, my class was once asked to bring in their most treasured possession and I brought my bible.

After leaving school I went on to study theology at university and ended up completing 5 years in 3 different locations. Even today, I make it a habit to read through the whole bible in a year, as well as studying it for preaching and teaching.

I heard a well-known minister once say that knowing and applying God's word will be what keeps God's people from falling into deception in the very last days. By ourselves, we are no match for the enemy, but armed with the unchanging truth of scripture we can combat and counteract every lie that comes from the pit of hell.

Make a fresh commitment to read, study, memorise and confess God's word on a regular basis and watch your faith grow as a result. "The grass withers and the flowers fall, but the word of our God endures forever." (Isaiah 40:8).

Prayer

Dear Father, thank you for giving us your word. I pray that it will become as important to me as the food I eat. Open my eyes to see fresh revelation from it and give me wisdom and understanding as I study it and apply it to my life. I pray this in Jesus' name, amen.

Day 25

0505 – Victory

Then one of the elders said to me, "Do not weep! See, the Lion of the tribe of Judah, the Root of David, has triumphed. He is able to open the scroll and its seven seals."
Revelation 5:5

We know that the number 5 represents grace and when I see 0505, I am reminded of the grace to overcome and walk in victory. In Revelation 5:5, John was upset that no-one was worthy enough to open the scroll that revealed the future of the world in the last days, but in the middle of his despair, he was told to stop weeping for Jesus – the Lion of Judah – had conquered and was able to do what no-one else could do.

1 John 5:4 echoes this statement of triumph when it says, "everyone born of God overcomes the world. This is the victory that has overcome the world, even our faith." Often in life, we face major challenges and obstacles which can rock our faith and cause us to panic. We might receive an alarming message or phone call or be given some bad news that we did not expect.

I've been in this position a number of times and although it is never easy to go through at the time, I've discovered that it's best to stay in peace and trust God that He will turn the situation around for good just like He has in the past.

This is not to say that we do not pray and look to the Lord for help. I believe our immediate response in times of crisis should be to run to God and pray believing that He will make a way and is already working on our behalf. We should also seek Him for a word or scripture that can speak into our situation.

Recently, I faced a challenge of my own and as I drove home praying about it, I asked the Holy Spirit to give me a word that dealt with what I was facing. Later that evening, I was led to Isaiah 49:25, which was exactly what I needed to hear and might be the very word you need to receive now or in the future.

The Easy-to-Read Version says: Here is the LORD's answer: "The prisoners will escape. Those captured by the strong soldier will be set free. That's because I will fight your battles, and I will save your children."

Prayer

Dear Lord, help me not to panic or despair in the light of negative news, but give me your grace to stay at peace and continue to walk in faith. Help me to see every situation from your perspective, which is one of victory and breakthrough. In Jesus' name, amen.

51

DAY 26

0606 – TIME TO PRAY

*But when you pray, go into your room, close
the door and pray to your Father, who is
unseen. Then your Father, who sees what is
done in secret, will reward you.*
John 6:6

Jesus didn't say "if you pray" but rather "when you pray." Prayer
for the believer is not an optional extra but a foundational building
block of the Christian faith. If we were to stop talking to one of our
family members, then our relationship with them would quickly
deteriorate and it's the same with God. We need prayer like a fish
needs water.

Whenever I see 0606, it's a reminder to pray. In fact, the apostle
Paul said we must "pray without ceasing" (2 Thessalonians 5:17).
This doesn't mean that we keep talking without stopping, but rather
we should always be aware of our communion with God and avoid
drifting into a state of prolonged prayerlessness.

Learning how to pray led to one of my biggest breakthroughs. It
came out of a desperation to see my circumstances change and as a
result, I discovered how to really cry out to God in the secret place.

Jesus knew the importance of starting the day in fellowship with
the Father, which is why He often retreated to lonely and isolated

places early in the morning before anyone was around. He knew that the secret of His strength wasn't in His title, gifting or ministry, but in abiding with God until He was full of the Holy Spirit and ready to help others.

Make it your goal to start scheduling time with the Lord. It may start off with just 15 minutes in the morning, but if you keep doing it then it will soon increase and before long, you'll be able to pray not just in the morning but all throughout the day at different times.

Prayer

Dear Father, thank you for the example of Jesus in teaching us how to pray and seek your face. I admit that I am weak without you, but with you I can do all things. I choose today to make time again to pray and spend time with you so that I can hear your voice more clearly and see what you're doing in the world. Help me to keep focused on this and not be distracted. In Jesus' name, amen.

DAY 27

0707 – ASK, SEEK, KNOCK

Ask and it will be given to you; seek and you will find; knock and the door will be opened to you. Matthew 7:7

When I see 0707, it is a reminder to be active in seeking God and His kingdom. It is not enough to just hope for things or wait until they suddenly appear in our lives, but there must be a proactive pursuit of what God has put in our hearts to achieve.

I am the kind of person who, when I really want to get something done, will keep pushing until it gets done. I remember seeing a vision of landscaping a garden of a house I had recently moved into which needed a lot of work. By the morning of the next day, I was already beginning to hire machinery and install new fencing and it wasn't long before the garden was transformed.

God wants us to be relentless in our search for Him and the promises He has made. I believe that He hides things for us as much as He hides things from us. The fact that Jesus tells us to knock on doors, means that they are there to be opened and entered and that the right ones will lead to good things.

We cannot afford to be passive Christians in this life and avoid bothering God with our requests either out of fear, ignorance or indifference. Matthew 7:11 encourages us that God wants to give good gifts to His children!

To receive what God has for us, Jesus tells us to do 3 things which require 3 different parts of our bodies. We are to ask with our mouths, seek with our eyes and knock with our hands. This shows that wants every part of us to be involved in the process.

Finally, be specific about what you want from the Lord and go in search for it. Ruth Graham made a list for what she wanted in a husband and when Billy Graham, the famous evangelist came along, she realised he ticked every box.

Prayer

Dear Father, please help me to keep asking, seeking and knocking as Jesus commanded us. You want us to give us good gifts and will release them when we continue to seek you. Increase my faith. In Jesus' name, amen.

DAY 28

2233 – PERFECT GUIDANCE

*God is my strength and power, And He makes
my way perfect.*
2 Samuel 22:33

Satellite navigation systems help us get to our destination quickly and accurately. They have almost completely replaced conventional paper maps. While they are generally correct and helpful, they are not entirely perfect and can sometimes take us off course!

God is the only one who can make our "way perfect" as the verse above illustrates.

When God made the world, He created everything perfect. It was sin that corrupted His creation and brought brokenness and imperfection. This is why Jesus came to the earth – to redeem us and all that God had made and restore it back to how it was meant to be.

One day we will be with the Lord in heaven and will have perfect bodies in a new and perfect world, but until then we are continually working towards this. God's ultimate plan is to make us whole and complete, lacking nothing. This is why we are being inwardly renewed day by day (2 Corinthians 4:16).

Although we will never achieve full perfection in this life, we are still called to strive towards it – to be holy, just as God is holy and to be mature and complete. Jesus was made perfect while he was alive through the suffering He endured and likewise our troubles and trials can be the very means to bring us closer to God and cause us to look to Him to make our way straight.

Prayer

Dear God, thank you for promising to guide me in all your ways and to lead me in paths of righteousness. Even when things don't work out and I feel lost or confused, I know that you can put me back on track and show me your good and perfect will in Christ Jesus, amen.

DAY 29

2244 – SEATED WITH CHRIST

The Lord said to my Lord, "Sit at My right hand, until I place Your enemies as a footstool for Your feet." Matthew 22:44

Where we sit is very important. It determines our position, status, friendships, work, home, attitude and more. The first verse of the first Psalm warns us against sitting with those who mock God's law. God is predominately depicted in the bible as sitting on a great throne watching over the whole earth.

Before we came to Christ, we walked and sat in darkness and sin. Now that we have been born-again, we have a new position and that is seated with Christ in heavenly places (Ephesians 2:6). This means we can look at situations from a different perspective – not as one looking up from the ground but as one looking down from above.

I once heard of a strategy from a businessman called the helicopter method. This involved imagining yourself in a helicopter looking down on your problems or challenges in order to see more clearly until you could figure out a solution or see things in a different light.

This is similar to what the bible encourages us to do when we see ourselves seated in high places with Jesus. We are not a defeated people begging God to come and rescue us all the time. We are a holy nation of kings and priests who have been given all power and authority to rule on this earth. When we see ourselves this way it changes how we pray and operate as believers.

It starts with sitting though. One of the most powerful spiritual exercises I've discovered in recent years is that of just sitting quietly and peacefully with Jesus – looking to Him and listening to His voice. Many prophetic words, visions and pictures have come from this posture.

Why don't you try it today? Find a quiet space where you will not be disturbed or distracted and simply sit with the Lord. Don't come with an agenda or prayer list but just make it your goal to abide with Him and let His love and presence overtake you. You will be surprised at the results and will be less aware of your problems and more aware of God.

Prayer

Dear Father, I choose to sit with you today and take my rightful place in heavenly places. Instead of running around frantically and anxiously, I make it my goal to abide with you until my enemies are under me rather than looming over me. Thank you that Jesus made this possible when He died on the cross for me. In His name, amen.

DAY 30

0321 – GET READY!

Therefore, keep watch, because you do not know the day or the hour.
Matthew 25:13

I recently had a strange experience. I woke up just before 2am and looked over at a radio clock that was in the room. It has always worked perfectly and never had any issues, but when I looked at it this time, all the hands had stopped a fraction before midnight. As I was trying to figure out why this had happened, suddenly the hands began to move quickly until they had caught up with the current time. At the same moment, a video notification popped up on my phone entitled "awake and sober!" If this wasn't enough, a few days later, I woke up and looked at the time and it was 3:21am!

There is absolutely no doubt that we are living in the last days. I believe the end of the world is right at the door and Jesus is about to come back at any moment. So many prophecies and promises are coming to pass that it is hard to keep up with them.

As believers, we know that Jesus is coming to rescue and redeem His people and His reward is with Him. As the world gets darker and more corrupt, the church is getting brighter as it stands out in the midst of wickedness and sin. The world might be going down, but we are going up and we want to take as many with us as possible.

It's time for the church to go into the darkness and rescue the lost. Jesus said, "As long as it is day, we must do the works of him who sent me. Night is coming, when no one can work" (John 9:4).

Right now, the church has an opportunity and open window to share the gospel to the ends of the earth. As I write this, outreaches are taking place around the world that are reaching millions of souls. Time is incredibly short and we want to do everything that God has planned for us to do before the door of the ark is shut.

I encourage you to make a fresh commitment to get back into prayer and God's presence and to make the most of every opportunity you have to tell others about what Jesus did for you and what He can do for them.

Prayer

Dear Father, I know that time is rapidly running out and I want to serve you wholeheartedly before you come again. Please help me to keep spiritually awake and watchful and to make the most of every opportunity you give me. Fill me with boldness and courage in these last days to stand for you and testify about you to others so that I will be unashamed at your return. In Jesus' name, amen.

Before you go...

Can I ask you one very important question: "Do you know Jesus?" If the answer is no then I would like to introduce you to Him. He is the Son of God and the Saviour of the world and He died on a cross for your sins 2000 years ago. He didn't come to judge us, but to save us through his death and resurrection.

Romans 10:13 says "Everyone who calls on the name of the Lord will be saved." I called to Jesus at the age of 5 and asked Him to forgive me of my sins, to make me clean and to live inside of me and that is exactly what He has done for almost 40 years.

If you do not have a relationship with Jesus then invite Him into your life today and start with this prayer:

Dear Jesus,

I admit that I am a sinner and need saving. I believe that only you can save me through your death and resurrection. I repent of my sins and turn away from them today. Please come into my heart and make me clean. Show me the path that you have for me and help me to walk on it with you for the rest of my life. I can only do this through the power of the Holy Spirit.

In your name,

Amen.

If you prayed that prayer then please get in touch with us and let us know as we would love to hear from you and celebrate your new journey in Christ. Go to citylights.org.uk to send us a message.

Finally, why not write down any other numbers you are seeing and appropriate bible verses at the back of this book and discover what God is trying to say to you.

Printed in Great Britain
by Amazon